Dr. Bernice Kastner received her BS Honors in Mathematics and Physics from McGill University in Montreal. She is a professor emeritus of Towson University, having received her Ph.D. in Math Education from the University of Maryland. Dr. Kastner has developed curriculum for Simon Fraser University in British Columbia, Montgomery College, the University of Maryland, and other universities.

Dr. Kastner's publications include:

- Study Guide: *Principles of Mathematics for Teachers*; Simon Fraser University, 2009

- Study Guide: *The Math Workshop: Algebra*; Simon Fraser University, 1989 (with Malgorzata Dubiel)

- *Space Mathematics:* A Resource for the Secondary School Teacher; NASA, 1986

- *Applications of Secondary School Mathematics*; National Council of Teachers of Mathematics, 1978

- 1979 Yearbook of the National Council of Teachers of Mathematics; *Applications in School Mathematics*; NCTM 1979 (Contributing author)

- *Unifying Concepts and Processes in Elementary Mathematics*; University of Maryland Mathematics Project; Allyn & Bacon, 1978 (Contributing author)

Articles:

- "Space Travel Angles"; *Quantum*, January/February 1992, Springer-Verlag
- "Number Sense: The Role of Measurement Applications"; *The Arithmetic Teacher*; February 1989

- "Decimal Fractions: The Case for Manipulatives"; *Vector*, BCAMT, Winter, 1988

- "Some Applications of Logarithms"; *Vector*, BCAMT Spring, 1985

Public Information:

- *U.S. School Mathematics from an International Perspective: A Guide for Speakers*; Mathematical Sciences Education Board of the National Research Council. National Academy Press, 1989 (Contributing author)

This book is dedicated to my lifelong friend Claire Bernstein, a lawyer, writer (*You Be the Judge*), and now a blogger (*To Life, With Love*) in my home town, Montreal, Quebec, Canada. She kept encouraging me to 'stick with it' every time I was ready to abandon this project.

Bernice Kastner

THE ROLE OF LANGUAGE IN TEACHING CHILDREN MATH

AUSTIN MACAULEY PUBLISHERS™

LONDON • CAMBRIDGE • NEW YORK • SHARJAH

Ordering Information:
Quantity sales: special discounts are available on quantity purchases by corporations, associations, and others. For details, contact the publisher at the address below.

Publisher's Cataloguing-in-Publication data
Kastner, Bernice
The Role of Language in Teaching Children Math

ISBN 9781641825429 (Paperback)
ISBN 9781641825436 (Hardback)
ISBN 9781641825443 (E-Book)

The main category of the book — Education / Teaching Methods & Materials / Mathematics

www.austinmacauley.com/us

First Published (2019)
Austin Macauley Publishers LLC
40 Wall Street, 28th Floor
New York, NY 10005
USA

mail-usa@austinmacauley.com
+1 (646) 5125767

First and foremost, I thank my children – Judith Skillman, Ruth E. Kastner, Joel Kastner – all of whom are writers in their respective fields (literature, philosophy of science, astronomy), for their constant encouragement and assistance as I have tried to make people in mathematics education aware of the importance of language and how it is used in the context of mathematics education. Thanks also to Tom Skillman for invaluable assistance with the diagrams and with format issues.

I am grateful to Malgorzata Dubiel of the Department of Mathematics at Simon Fraser University (Burnaby, British Columbia, Canada) and Melania Alvarez at the Pacific Institute of Mathematical Sciences (Vancouver, British Columbia, Canada), for offering me the opportunity to participate in and look closely at the current preparation offered to elementary school teachers and at what is taught in elementary school mathematics.

I thank Deborah Halperin, recipient of the President's Award for Excellence in Mathematics Teaching 2014, and Virginia (Gini) Stimpson of the mathematics education group at the University of Washington, Seattle, for some stimulating discussions and for providing me with current copies of elementary school mathematics textbooks.

Thanks also to fellow Horizon House (Seattle, WA) residents, Patricia Henry, Nancy Robinson, and Phyllis Van Orden, for reading early drafts and providing helpful feedback.

Table of Contents

Preface

Recent research has shown that some important aspects of human number sense are actually inborn (Dehaene; Carey et al; Buttersworth), and that the language processing capabilities of the human brain are very much involved in mathematical activity. The implications of this research for the teaching and learning of mathematics are profound.

There is also a well-established myth that the verbal and symbolic language of mathematics is clear and unambiguous, but in fact no human language has such properties. If we fear confusing children by showing them that mathematical words and symbols can have different meanings, we should consider whether we might be promoting more serious confusion and misunderstanding by denying or obscuring this reality.

Every school-age child has already become proficient in his or her native language, even though that language has words that have different meanings in different contexts as well as different words for a given object or action. Why do we think children will be unable to handle these same features in the language of math? If we were to address the ambiguities and subtleties, instead of pretending they do not exist, we could avoid creating the kind of self-doubt that can make a learner feel stupid, when the problem actually lies in the language rather than in the student.

We must also be aware that once words have been attached to concepts, there is a tendency for those words to "stick" even after the ideas have been further developed and the words no longer actually describe the new understanding.

For example, we talk about "real" and "imaginary" numbers in mathematics; historically, "real numbers" were considered to be properties of concrete aspects of the world. Mathematics has developed far beyond those original ideas, and the Oxford Dictionary now defines mathematics itself as "the abstract science of number, quantity, and space." All numbers are now recognized as abstractions, and the terms "real number" and "imaginary number" are anachronisms.

In fact, mathematics is so very powerful *because* it is rooted in abstractions; once a mathematical tool is developed to solve a particular problem in a specific area, it can often be applied in other contexts. For example, the Scottish mathematician and inventor John Napier (1550–1617) developed the idea of the logarithm in response to the need to more efficiently perform the very cumbersome work required for multiplication and division after the invention of the telescope expanded human ability to measure much greater distances in astronomy. He also proposed the use of the decimal point as another way to represent fractions that extends the base-ten aspect of our number system, and he showed that the associated computational procedures would be less tedious than those in use at that time. As we all know, decimal representation for fractions has indeed been useful and is now the preferred method for fraction computation.

Napier's legacy of the logarithm has been valuable in far more ways than making computation faster and easier. For example, once mathematicians and scientists became familiar with this function, people working in fields such as physiology were able to recognize that, in fact, many human senses (as well as other phenomena of the natural world) operate in a logarithmic way.

It is well past time to address the fact that we have to think in terms of much more challenging goals for mathematics education. While it may once have been important to society that school children be trained to become efficient "calculating machines," such machines now exist and well outperform any human calculation efforts (Stanislas Dehaene. *The Number Sense,* 2011).

The urgent task of our educational system must be to ensure that students understand and can correctly use the language and procedures of mathematics that go far beyond computational skill. This requires explicit acknowledgement of the existence of multiple interpretations of verbal and symbolic mathematical language.

The great British mathematical psychologist, Richard R. Skemp, published a paper in the journal *Mathematics Teaching (1976), Relational Understanding and Instrumental Understanding.* He pointed out that teaching strategies used in mathematics could be compared with trying to teach someone to play the piano by starting with a cardboard keyboard (i.e., unable to hear any music). His influence was profound but not always understood, since it seems that students now emerge from our schools so lacking in any kind of understanding that we are told it is unreasonable to require competence in algebra for entry to post-secondary education (Hacker, others).

Human societies are cultural in nature and use language to share, communicate, and record information. This is apparently a survival skill that has contributed to the progressive development of our species. But it is clear that human languages are not precise unambiguous conveyers of meaning in any area of communication.

This book shows some of the ways in which current mathematics curriculum materials, beginning in the early grades, fail to provide students with the kind of understanding they need in order to deal with the unavoidable verbal and symbolic language issues which are inherent in trying to convey abstract meanings. We will also show how the history of the development of some aspects of the subject has led to current student misconceptions, and suggest viable strategies to help students become empowered, rather than to feel that they are not smart enough to learn mathematics.

Chapter 1
Different Meanings for Mathematical Terms and Symbols

Lewis Carroll:
> "When I use a word," Humpty Dumpty said in a rather scornful tone, "it means just what I choose it to mean, neither more nor less."
> "The question is," said Alice, "whether you can make words mean different things."
> "The question is," said Humpty Dumpty, "which is to be master – that's all."

Can you think of an English word that has more than one meaning? This should not be very difficult. If you open any dictionary at random, you will probably see many such words. I did this with my dictionary (Webster's Ninth New Collegiate Dictionary, 1989) and found three different listings for the word "high," as adjective, adverb, and noun. Each of these had several meanings – in fact, there were eleven just for the adjective. The situation for the verbal and symbolic language of mathematics is very similar, even though mathematicians work hard to form clear definitions.

English Number Words

Before examining some of the different meanings of mathematical terminology, it may be useful to give some attention to the words used in the English language to name numbers. Although it was not always so, number systems are now universally based on grouping by tens and powers of ten;

in other words, we use a base-ten system. Historical records show that at various times and in various places, other groupings were used, such as 12, 20, and 60. Relics of these other groupings are still evident: we sell eggs by the dozen; the quantity "score" means 20 and the French word for 80 is "quatre-vingt (four twenties); there are 60 minutes in an hour and 60 seconds in a minute.

One unfortunate feature of the English language (as well as several other western European languages), is that the *words* used for the smaller two-digit numbers do not transparently reveal the fact that we are grouping in tens. In contrast, for most eastern European and Asian languages, numbers larger than ten *explicitly* state the number of tens and the number of ones. Few people know that the etymology of the word "eleven" is "one left" (i.e., one more than ten) and that of "twelve" is "two left." When we count in English, the words after ten are eleven and twelve, followed by thirteen, fourteen... The "teen" words tell how many ones there are in addition to the base of ten, with the number of ones stated first. The word for two tens is "twenty" and from then on, the words change pattern to tell first how many tens there are, and then how many ones.

For young children who are just learning to count, the languages whose words for numbers greater than ten explicitly mean ten and one, ten and two, ten and three... ten and nine, followed by two tens and one, two tens and two, etc., clearly reveal the base-ten structure of the number system. Since the fact that we are grouping by tens is not obvious in English number words, it is extremely important for the early mathematics curriculum to make children aware that the symbol 12 is shorthand for "ten and two" because this is not revealed by the word "twelve." I have personally had the experience of being asked by one of my grandchildren, then four years old, "Grandma, why does twelve have a one and a two?"

The table below shows how the structure of the base-ten nature of the number system is more transparent in the number words used by the Mandarin Chinese and Czech languages than in the English language. Notice also that the Chinese number words are quite explicit: "twelve" is "ten-two" (implying ten and two) and "twenty-two" is "two-ten-two" (implying two tens and two). The Czech words, while slightly less direct, still literally show that what is being counted is groups of tens and how many additional ones.

Numeral	English	Mandarin	Czech
1	one	yi	jedna
2	two	er	dve
3	three	san	tri
4	four	si	ctyri
5	five	wu	pet
6	six	liu	sest
7	seven	qi	sedm
8	eight	ba	osm
9	nine	jiu	devet
10	ten	shi	deset
11	eleven	shiyi	jedenact
12	twelve	shier	dvanact
13	thirteen	shisan	trinact
14	fourteen	shisi	ctrnact
15	fifteen	shiwu	patnact
16	sixteen	shliu	sestnact
17	seventeen	shiqi	sedmnact
18	eighteen	shiba	osmnact
19	nineteen	shijiu	devatnact
20	twenty	ershi	dvacet
21	twenty-one	ershiyu	dvacet jedna
22	twenty-two	ershier	dvacet dva
23	twenty-three	ershisan	dvacet tre

| 24 | twenty-four | ershisi | dvacet ctyri |
| 25 | twenty-five | ershiwu | dvacet pet |

We obscure the base-ten nature of the number system even more by the language we use when teaching the standard algorithms for addition, subtraction, and multiplication of multi-digit numbers. Children are shown when and how to "carry one" in addition or "borrow one" in subtraction, and how to offset alignment of the partial products in multiplication. However, the "one" that is being "carried" in the addition algorithm never actually means one – it is always a power of ten: "one ten" or "one hundred" or "one thousand," etc., depending on the column in which it is placed. In cultures where the abacus is used, or has been used relatively recently, it is much easier for the learner to appreciate the subtlety of saying "one" when what is meant is ten, one hundred, or one thousand. When the visual model of the abacus is familiar, the value of "one bead" of an abacus depends on which wire holds that bead.

While most children eventually master these algorithms, confidence is easily undermined when the focus is on rote learning of a meaningless procedure. Modern teaching materials use the language of "regrouping" instead of "carry one" or "borrow one," but misleading language anachronisms are remarkably resilient. Stanislas Dehaene has also pointed out, in his book *The Number Sense*, that the fact that Chinese number words are short creates a smaller burden on short-term memory, making it much easier for children to learn and remember multiplication facts. His research has also shown how much more difficult it is for children to master arithmetic in cultures (such as Welsh) that have long, complicated number words.

The meaning of the word "number"

The word "number" has many meanings, as can be seen in any dictionary. My own dictionary has seven different entries for "number" as a noun, each with subsections. Some, but not all, of the meanings are mathematical. However, the usage of this word in the context of mathematics has changed over the millennia. The ancient Greeks distinguished between the kinds of numbers used to count *discrete,* or separable objects (multitudes), and those used to compare physical characteristics of *continuous* objects, with characteristics like length or area or mass (magnitudes), which we now call measurements. Using ratios to compare groups with respect to how many members were in each group was seen as part of the "multitude" idea. Now we use the same word "number" for situations involving discrete objects, for ratios, and for measurements.

There is, however, a fundamental difference between counting discrete objects and measuring physically continuous characteristics. Measurement is based on comparing whatever is to be measured with a chosen standard: the unit. Counting is involved, but what we count are *copies of the* unit, as well as *equal subdivisions of the unit* that has been chosen as a standard for the measurement, when we see that a whole number of copies of the unit does not provide as much information as we want. Every measurement involves a "best fit" *judgment* about how many standard units and parts of the unit are needed to match what is being measured.

Historically, the situation was further complicated after it was recognized (via the Pythagorean Theorem) that side lengths of a triangle can be "incommensurable." For example, the length of the hypotenuse of an isosceles right triangle cannot be expressed exactly in terms of any fractional part of the unit that measures the two equal sides. Greek mathematics continued to develop power by acknowledging the distinction between the numbers that arise in geometric contexts (magnitudes) and those that emerge from counting (multitudes).

It would probably not matter that the language used in mathematics no longer reveals the distinction between the kinds of numbers that arise in discrete contexts and those that arise in continuous contexts if our instructional practices would help children understand that these are in fact *conceptually* different kinds of numbers. One fascinating outcome of recent research (Dehaene, Carey) is that humans are actually born with two different kinds of number senses: the one for size is very different than the one for discriminating and enumerating discrete objects. The research has shown that very young infants (as well as some animals) are able to distinguish the differences between 1, 2, or 3 separate objects or people. It appears that we also have an intrinsic way to think of joining small sets of discrete objects, an "accumulator." However, the sense of "size," – often involving judgments about magnitudes – operates quite differently. For example, we see the difference between 68 and 70 as much smaller than the difference between 8 and 10. A mathematician would describe the "magnitude number sense" as logarithmic rather than linear.

Unfortunately, the way we teach measurement in our schools today obscures the distinction between "multitude" numbers and "magnitude" numbers, by treating measurements as though they are known *exactly*. If we taught children to measure by having them perform simple real-world measurements of length, capacity, or weight using actual rulers, measuring cups, and balance scales, they would immediately confront and have to deal with the fact that no measurement can be exact. Every measurement has a built-in "error" due to the necessity for "best fit" judgments. Measurement error can be reduced with the use of precision tools, but can never be entirely eliminated. Our teaching materials in the early grades, instead of having children make actual measurements – a useful skill – present contrived pictures in which measurements *appear to be* exact whole numbers or exactly match whatever fractional units are on the measuring device. Figure 1.1 below is typical of what is seen in textbooks.

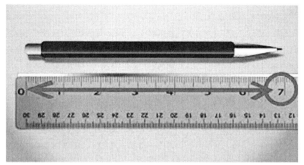

Figure 1.1

We need to be aware that it is rare to find an exact whole number measurement when a pencil is placed next to a ruler, and it can do more harm than good to avoid the reality of measurement error. We will return to this issue in the context of rational numbers, since American students continue to be severely hampered with respect to developing mastery of operations with rational numbers, as shown in international tests and by research studies such as the one by Siegler and Lortie-Forges cited in Chapter 2.

The meaning of the word "angle"

The context in which elementary school children are introduced to angles is geometry, where an angle is usually defined as a set of points consisting of a point *P* and two rays extending from *P*. The point *P* is the *vertex* and the rays are the *sides* of the angle. There are variations in this definition; sometimes it is required that the two rays not lie along the same straight line, to prevent the confusion inherent in the term "straight angle" which some people use when the two rays happen to lie on the same line but point in opposite directions.

We need to question the wisdom of offering such a definition. While it is indeed appropriate for formal point-set geometry, it seems counter-productive in the context of what young children are asked to learn about angles, namely their identification, description, and measurement. The intuitive ideas about angles are better captured in the common dictionary definition as "the space (usually measured in degrees) between two intersecting lines at or close to the point where they meet" – what would be called the *interior* of the angle under the point-set definition.

Many elementary school teachers feel vaguely insecure about what the word "angle" means, and their students inevitably feel insecure as well. What young children are expected to learn about angles is how to identify, describe, and measure them. The focus is not on the rays but on what most dictionary definitions of angle say: "the space (usually measured in degrees) between two intersecting lines at or close to the point where they meet" – what would be called the *interior* of the angle under the definition using rays. The two parts of figure 1.2 below illustrate the ideas of the different approaches to the meaning of "angle."

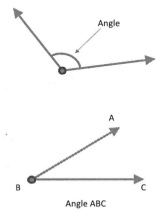

Figure 1.2 (a) and (b)

Later in their schooling, students who study trigonometry will learn about "directed angles" in terms of rotating a ray counter-clockwise from an initial staring point to a final resting place, which is closer to the intuition developed through measurement. Because of the visual nature of any work with angles most students "figure it out." For those who do not, it's important to understand that in fact the language is confusing.

As an interesting aside, the angle measurement context can provide an opportunity for students to learn about the history of mathematics and the development of numeration systems. Angle measurement has retained the historical use of base 60; the subdivisions of the degree, the unit used for angle measurement, are *minutes* and *seconds*, as is also the case for the hour in the measurement of time: there are 60 seconds in a minute, and 60 minutes in a degree (or in an hour, for time). The words "minute" and "second" are in fact derived from the Latin translations of early measurements that used base-60 for the number system and for subdivisions of the fundamental units: "*partes minutiae*" (little parts) and "*partes minutiae secundae*" (second little parts).

Some early civilizations used calendars based on a 360-day year, which is why the degree is defined so that a complete revolution has 360 degrees. Historical records show that adjustments were made as needed, in an "ad hoc" manner, to keep those calendars from departing too far from the expected seasons, a strategy still seen in our present use of "leap years" for the same purpose. However, it was also necessary for the people who were responsible for those calendars to use a base number with many divisors in order to be able to do the necessary calculations in the absence of computational methods we now take for granted. Note that our familiar number symbols, as well as fraction notation, were only developed during the period of 800-1500 years ago.

Although young children are not expected to measure angles more precisely than the nearest degree, this context provides another opportunity to focus on the distinction between counting discrete objects and measuring continuous properties so that children may learn that we cannot expect measurement to produce exact numbers.

Mathematical symbols with multiple interpretations

Just as every human spoken language uses the same sounds to mean different things in different contexts, the symbolic language of mathematics reuses symbols. Sometimes the different meanings are related but sometimes they are not, and the existence of such differences can create real problems for the learner. Here are some examples, ranging from relatively elementary to very sophisticated levels of mathematics:

1. The minus sign: (-) has three distinct meanings:

- When it is between two numbers or expressions, it is the symbol for the operation of subtraction: 5 - 2 is an instruction to subtract 2 from 5.

- When it is in front of a number, the number is being designated as negative and no arithmetic operation is involved. For example, -6 is a negative number.

- When it is in front of a letter, it designates an additive inverse: -a is the value that must be added to the value of a to produce 0.

Most people (including many college graduates) don't seem to recognize that we can't know if the number represented by -a is positive or negative unless we know whether a itself is a positive or negative number: If a is positive, then -a is negative, but if a is a negative number, then -a is positive. Teachers need to find out if their students have developed an automatic reaction to interpret a minus sign in front of a *symbol* as designating a negative number, and actively work with those students to overcome this mindless automatic response. I always had many such students at the college level, as well as in secondary school.

2. The symbol 0, called "zero," has three rather different roles:

- "0" is used as a placeholder in our base-ten number system. We know that the numeral 204 means there are 2 hundreds, no tens, and 4 ones. There are historical relics (clay tablets) of the early Mesopotamian numeration system that used base 60 but had no placeholder symbol. Historians attempting to decipher these relics must find other cues, if any are available, to determine the actual value for what is clearly a numeral. Without knowing the context that produced the number that is shown as the symbol for "5" followed by the symbol for "3" in Mesopotamian symbols it can be impossible to determine whether the intended number is $[5(60)^2 + 3]$ or $[5(60) + 3]$.

- "0" is used to designate the whole number that shows how many elements are in an empty set. It is unfortunate that children are permitted, even encouraged, to say that zero is "nothing" when it is in this role. However, it is still a *number,* and in fact *every number* is an abstraction, and so could be seen as "nothing" of any substance. While I may hold up two fingers or have two children stand up to illustrate the number "two," the eventual goal is for children to understand that "two" is the property shared by all sets of two objects.

- It is the additive identity for the integers, the rational numbers, and the real numbers. This means that it has no effect when added: $n + 0 = 0 + n = n$ for any number n. The additive identity is a special number and has important properties in

25

multiplication and division. If students believe that zero is "nothing," there is no conceptual foundation with which to understand why 0 multiplied by any number is still 0, or why we can never divide by 0.

3. The same symbol is sometimes used to represent a fraction and sometimes to represent a ratio. Ratios are used to make comparisons, and until relatively recently it was traditional to represent a ratio comparison with a colon (:). For example, if a certain bead pattern has 5 white beads for every 8 beads, this ratio of 5 to 8 would be written as 5:8. It is now more common to write such a ratio as $\frac{5}{8}$, exactly the same way as for the fraction. However, ratios and fractions have different meanings and do not use the same kind of arithmetic. This issue will be discussed further in Chapter 2.

4. Parentheses mean different things in different contexts. Here are three different uses (involving different meanings) of these symbols:

- The parentheses might designate multiplication: for example
  $$2(-4) = 2 \times (-4) = -8$$

- They might be part of function notation such as $f(x)$, where the letter before the parentheses simply names the function, and the letter between the parentheses names the variable in the function for which numbers can be substituted.

- They might be part of an instruction to substitute a specific number for the variable in a previously defined function: For the function
  $$f(x) = x^2 - 5,$$
  $$f(2) = 2^2 - 5 = 4 - 5 = -1$$

5. There are different meanings for symbols such as $(3, 5)$ or (a, b), parentheses surrounding two letters or numbers separated by a comma. In mathematics, this symbol is used in connection with each of the following conceptually very different entities:

- An open interval on the number line

- The coordinates of a point in the plane

- An "ordered pair" in a relationship that connects the first element to the second

If the context is available, there is usually no problem of interpretation. However, it is important to be aware that without a context there is no way to know what meaning is intended for the symbol. It would also be helpful to students if we would explicitly acknowledge that this same symbol has different interpretations in different contexts.

6. In algebra, a letter is often used to represent an "unknown." Sometimes this "unknown" is a variable that can have different values, but sometimes it is a constant that can only have one value (which may or may not be known). By convention, variables are often represented by letters that are at the end of our alphabet, while constants are usually represented by letters at the beginning or in the middle of the alphabet. For most beginning algebra students, such conventions are rarely discussed and letters are simply seen as variables.

7. The word "term" has different meanings in different contexts. A term of a *fraction* is the numerator or denominator, and when the numerator and denominator have no common factor, we say the fraction is in *lowest terms*. A term of a *proportion* such as a:b::c:d is any one of the extremes (a or d) or the means (b or c). A term of an *equation* or *inequality* is the entire quantity on one side of the "equal," "less than," or "more than" sign. For an *expression* that involves sums and/or differences of several quantities, each of those quantities is referred to as a term.

8. The exponent (-1) has two very different interpretations. This can be a serious source of trouble but it is rarely discussed explicitly.

- In some contexts, it means a reciprocal: $x^{-1} = \frac{1}{x}$.

- It is also used to designate an inverse function:

  When $f(x) = y$, then $f^{-1}(y) = x$.

  Or: $\sin^{-1} p = q$ means that $\sin q = p$

  NOTICE that $\sin^{-1} p$ does NOT mean $\frac{1}{\sin p}$.

9. There are two different kinds of notation used for the derivative in calculus. For a function $y = f(x)$, the derivative may be written as $f'(x)$ or as $\frac{dy}{dx}$. The symbol $\frac{dy}{dx}$ is not considered to be a fraction, since it is defined as the *limit* of the difference quotient $\frac{\Delta y}{\Delta x}$ as the variable x approaches zero, and this implies that the numerator and denominator are not to be separated. However, in the context of differentials, the quantities dy and dx are in fact separated.

Chapter 2
Different Names or Symbols for the Same Concept

William Shakespeare:
>"What's in a name? That which we call a rose
>By any other name would smell as sweet."

It's easy enough to agree that for physical objects, such as roses, it may not matter what name is used to discuss them. In the world of mathematics, however, we deal with abstractions. Numbers and geometric objects are *based on* real-world experience, but in mathematics, they are idealized concepts. We may hold up two fingers or ask two children to stand up to exemplify the number 2, but the number "2" itself is an abstract *idea* about the property shared by all sets of two objects. A geometric point has no size but when we use a dot on a sheet of paper to represent a location, the dot does have size. As discussed in Chapter 1, we now know that there is a profound conceptual difference, which appears to be inborn, between "2" as a count involving discrete objects (a "multitude") and "2 units" as a measure of some physical aspect of a real-world object (a "magnitude").

Fractions

Most children have not yet made the transition from the concrete to the abstract at the time fractions appear in the mathematics curriculum. Furthermore, unless they have had substantial experience with real-world measurement, the importance of the role of the unit being used for measuring (as well as its subdivisions), may not yet be sufficiently apparent for them to handle the subtleties of fraction notation. The history of mathematics shows that the development of the kind of symbolic representation that made it possible to easily perform computations involving fractions was long and difficult, and we need to realize that our teaching strategies have to provide opportunities for children to learn about the abstract nature of numbers. Recent research (Siegler and Lortie-Forgues, *Current Directions in Psychological Science,* 2017, Vol. 26(4), 346–351) confirms that children find it difficult to develop computational skill with fractions when there is no understanding of the nature of fractional numbers and the emphasis is on rote manipulation of meaningless symbols. The study also discusses the effect of language on providing meaning for fractional words and symbols by showing how the words used for fractions in East Asian languages such as Chinese, Japanese and Korean correspond to pictorial representations of such fractions.

We now commonly use two different kinds of symbolic representations for fractions: the decimal form and the fraction bar form. Once people developed the ability to measure by comparison with chosen unit standards, they soon realized the value of being able to make "better" (i.e., more precise) measurements by subdividing the unit of measurement. In other words, it was recognized that we could measure smaller things of the same nature, or things that obviously don't match a whole number of copies of the standard measuring unit, by breaking that unit into equal parts.

The fraction bar form came from this measurement context. It is based on the idea of subdividing the unit into equally sized parts, and then counting how many of these smaller parts are needed for a more precise measurement. The number of equal subdivisions of the unit is placed below the fraction bar (the denominator of the fraction) and the number of pieces required in order to match what is being measured is placed above the fraction bar (the numerator).

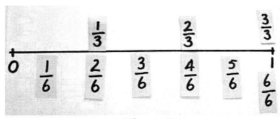

Figure 2.1

Most young children in the USA get their early experience in measuring length by using a foot-long ruler subdivided into 12 inches; the inch-long segments are sometimes subdivided into 4, 8, or 16 parts to obtain more precise measurements. These awkward fractions are the heritage of the British Imperial units of earlier centuries, which are no longer used by any industrialized country in the world, other than the USA.

The decimal form of fraction notation was based on an extension of our base-ten number system, where we name numbers in terms of groupings of tens and powers of ten. In this system, it is natural to break the unit into ten equal parts (tenths of the unit); each of these parts can again be subdivided into ten equal parts, or hundredths of the original unit, and this process can be repeated as long as we are able to manage the technical demands of this kind of subdivision. The metric units of measurement were developed in order to be able to take advantage of the base-ten system for numbers.

One of the problems in working with fractions comes from the difficulty of converting between these two forms in common use. To express a fraction such as $\frac{1}{6}$ or $\frac{3}{7}$ as a decimal, we divide the denominator into the numerator: $\frac{1}{6}$ becomes 0.16666… and $\frac{3}{7}$ becomes 0.4285714285714… Notice that fractions such as these do not have terminating decimal representations. In fact, since the only whole numbers that divide 10 evenly are 2 and 5, any fraction whose denominator has factors other than 2 and 5 will not terminate and have to be "rounded" somehow if we want to express it as a decimal number. It is likely that one reason for the historical use of number bases such as 60 and 12 in early eras (when the need for calculating was just beginning to be recognized), is that those numbers have more whole number divisors than 10 does. Handling "parts" of a quantity is much easier when there is a systematic way to express those parts. There is a lot of controversy now about calculator usage in school, but it has been my own experience that mindless drill on procedures such as the long division algorithm was no better for most children in terms of competence in mathematics. A more effective strategy is to teach for understanding.

We need to recognize the serious issues children must deal with, in order to understand and manipulate fractions, when techniques are taught before the children have had enough experience with measurement to understand the concept of a unit and the need to subdivide a unit. Without such background, it can be impossible to understand why it is necessary to express fractions with a common denominator in order to add or subtract them. In the United States, where Imperial units have not been replaced by the metric system, the complications are further increased because subdivisions of the "standard" measurement units are arbitrary and clumsy. As a result, it takes a lot of tedious calculation to express fractions in terms of a common denominator when it is necessary to add or subtract with fractions.

We will discuss the operations of arithmetic in Chapter 3. With respect to measured numbers, we fail to acknowledge the fact that the unit used to obtain the measurement is an inherent part of the *value* of the measured number: 2 m, 2 cm, 2 seconds, and 2 hours are very different measurements even though the same number is involved in each measure. When applying arithmetic in measurement contexts, our curriculum materials give very little attention to the units involved, and children are simply expected to append the "correct" unit to the numerical result after completing whatever computation is required. What is not clear is how we expect students to understand what the "correct" unit is.

Figure 2.2 illustrates what many students are led to think is a completely reasonable measurement: the pencil appears to exactly fit between marked points on the "number line," and no unit of measurement is given.

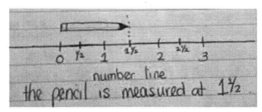

Figure 2.2

In fact, the *nature* of the geometric or physical quantities being measured is a part of the meaning embedded in the unit, and such numbers are described as *denominate numbers*. It is worth noting that in some other countries (whose children outperform Americans on the international tests), the mathematics curriculum involving the teaching of multiplication explicitly points out that when two *denominate* numbers, are multiplied, the unit of the product is *never* the same as the unit of *either* factor.

Given the fact that our language no longer shows the distinction between the kinds of numbers useful for counting and those needed for measuring, it is extremely important that we provide meaningful measurement experiences for our young students to help them understand the nature of measured numbers ("magnitudes") as discussed in the previous chapter. Unfortunately, we make such understanding even more elusive due to the way our children are taught decimal arithmetic techniques, where we seem to *deliberately* avoid any discussion of the fundamentally approximate nature of measurements. Instead, we consistently teach computational "rules" that students will eventually have to unlearn if they are to succeed in any area involving measured numbers, whether in science, carpentry, manufacturing, or engineering.

Calculations with decimal numbers are usually based on what appear to be real-world situations, but we teach children to treat numbers that are obviously measurements as though they were exact. Here are some examples of procedures we require students to mindlessly practice until they become habitual:

- In the context of addition and subtraction, children are routinely told to append zeros to the right of the decimal point when "ragged decimals" appear. For example, we ask children to add numbers such as 33 and 0.15, and teach them to append zeros to the whole number and then add 33.00 and 0.15 and present the sum as 33.15. However, if we ever genuinely need to add 33 and 0.15, a better answer might be 33 rather than 33.15. If the "33" was obtained by measuring only to the nearest unit, then a more accurate measuring tool might produce a value somewhere between 32.5 and 33.5. There are very few real-world situations, other than those involving money, that require such a sum to be performed. An actual measurement reported as 33 must be judged as having been measured to the nearest unit, so the replacement with 33.00 cannot be justified. While it is important to teach children to recognize and deal with "ragged decimals," it is not advisable to teach them to mindlessly append zeros to the right of a decimal point.

For example, here is a problem in a 2015 Grade 5 textbook (Pearson's "Envision Math" p. 45, #25):

A balloon mural of the Chicago Skyline measures 17.6 m on two sides and 26.21 m on the other two sides. What is the perimeter of the mural?

This is a "fake" real-world problem that provides an artificially created case of "ragged decimals" in order to support the lesson on aligning decimal points in addition. It requires the solver to append a zero to the 17.6 to obtain 17.60 because the other addend is expressed in hundredths. But if the longer sides could be measured to the nearest hundredth of a meter, then there is every reason to believe the shorter sides could also be measured with the same precision; if in fact the digit in the hundredths place for the shorter side had been observed as 0, the measurement should have been reported as 17.60 m. We should not be teaching children that it is acceptable to append zeros at will to actual measurements because if they ever do carpentry or study science they will have to "unlearn" such strategies.

- When multiplying measurements, we routinely teach students to retain all decimal places, thereby, consolidating the incorrect idea that all the digits are meaningful. To calculate the area of a rectangle whose length is 6.3 cm and width is 4.5 cm, the textbooks will say that the area is 28.35 cm^2. In fact, any length between 6.25 cm and 6.35 cm would be observed as 6.3 cm if the measurements were made with a ruler whose closest markings are tenths of a cm. As shown by the thick boundary in Figure 2.3 below, this means that the actual area of the rectangle would have a value somewhere between 27.81 cm^2 (6.25 x 4.45) and 28.89 cm^2 (6.35 x 4.55).

Figure 2.3

It is not actually difficult for children who have had experience with making real measurements to learn the "rule of thumb," that the product of two measured numbers should be given with no more significant digits than those of the measured numbers. In this example, we should report the area as 28 cm^2 because each of the original measurements only has two significant digits.

- For division, where the quotient is often a repeating decimal, textbooks usually advise children to give the answer to the nearest tenth or hundredth – a strategy to deal with the repeating decimal digits that completely ignores the issue of measurement error. Some texts provide a "rule" that says that the number of decimal places in the quotient should match the number of decimal places in the dividend. This "rule" will eventually have to be unlearned, since in practice what is meaningful for the computation is not the number of decimal places in either the divisor or the dividend, but the smallest number of significant digits in either measurement.

Perhaps more importantly, children who have had experience making actual measurements easily learn that while the "2" in a measurement such as 2 meters (2 m) may *look like* a whole number, this is only because of the unit chosen to report the measurement. Conventions have been established to provide information about how a measurement has been made, so that anyone using the measured numbers will have an estimate of the inherent error. If the length of an object has been measured to the nearest decimeter and has been found to be 20 decimeters (dm) long, convention requires that the length be reported either as 20 dm or 2.0 m. Part of the information in a measurement reported as 2 m (rather than 2.0 m) is that the measurement was made to the nearest meter. If the actual length is somewhere between 1.5 and 2.5 m but we are only able to measure to the nearest meter, the length would be given as 2 m.

We will discuss the operations of arithmetic in Chapter 3. With respect to measured numbers, we fail to acknowledge the fact that the unit used to obtain the measurement is an *inherent part* of the *value* of the measured number: 2 m, 2 cm, 2 seconds, and 2 hours are very different measurements, even though the same number is involved in each measure. The *nature* of the geometric or physical quantities being measured is a part of the meaning embedded in the unit, and such numbers are described as *denominate numbers*. It is worth noting that in some other countries (whose children outperform Americans on the international tests), the mathematics curriculum involving the teaching of multiplication explicitly points out that when two *denominate* numbers, are multiplied, the unit of the product is never the same as the unit of *either* factor.

Before the era of the calculator and computer, it was considered necessary to train people to be efficient calculating "machines," whether or not they understood what the calculations were about. Now that we have machines that easily outperform any human being in mindless computation, it has become even more important for people to be aware of how output from such devices will be used and interpreted. This requires people to have enough experience to recognize that measurements can't be treated as "pure" numbers and that the difference in measurements like 2 cm and 2.0 cm cannot simply be ignored. In an age when we claim that students are being prepared for competence in STEM (Science, Technology, Engineering, Mathematics) subjects, we must stop ignoring the vital distinction between measured numbers and counting numbers.

In fact, it is not sensible to report all decimal places showing on a calculator display when there can only be two significant digits. In addition, incorrect machine output can occur because of input or keystroke errors, and institutions such as banks require machine printouts in order to be able to track down such errors. We need human brain-power to be engaged in mathematical activity more than ever in today's world. We can and should teach students to perform mental calculations and estimations to anticipate the approximate machine outputs as a matter of habit. Printouts have shown how frequently digits are reversed (an entry of 17 can appear as 71) or a digit of a multi-digit number is omitted during entry.

To add to these issues, the only interpretation for multiplication that most children are taught is repeated addition. How can multiplication be understood as repeated addition in the context of denominate numbers or when both factors are fractions? If children are expected to make sense of arithmetic and its operations, we need to provide them with information about the multiple meanings actually given to these operations. The next chapter will focus on some of these meanings.

Another serious conceptual issue has developed in connection with fractions because of the relatively recent adoption of fraction bar notation to show a ratio comparison. For example, a statement such as "The ratio of boys to girls in Mr. Smith's class is 5 to 3," which at one time would have used colon notation and represented symbolically as 5:3, is now commonly shown as the fraction $\frac{5}{3}$. The statement itself is a proportion, and was formerly expressed as b:g::5:3, where b represents the number of boys and g the number of girls in Mr. Smith's class. It is now more common to state this kind of proportion as $\frac{b}{g} = \frac{5}{3}$.

But the world of ratios uses a different kind of arithmetic, which may be playfully described as "baseball arithmetic." In the sport of baseball, a player's batting average is the ratio of the number of hits to the number of turns at bat, converted to decimal notation. In sequential games, the number of hits and the number of turns at bat are simply accumulated. This means that as the playing season progresses, the ratio changes by a procedure where, if the ratio is expressed using the fraction bar, the numerators are added and the denominators are added to get the new ratio. This is exactly what many children want to do when there is no conceptual foundation for rational numbers as measurements.

A teacher's management of quiz scores may sometimes provide another context where children encounter the practice of adding "numerators" and adding "denominators" of what are actually ratios, rather than fractions. For a sequence of quizzes with varying numbers of questions, a student who correctly answers 3 of 5 questions on the first quiz, 6 of 8 questions on the second, and 4 of 7 questions on the third, will have an accumulated score of 13 out of 20.

Unfortunately, many current North American textbooks introduce fractions using set examples: for a set of 5 poker chips of which 2 are red, the children are expected to observe that $\frac{2}{5}$ of the set is red. While sets may be intuitively appealing in terms of *visualizing* "fractional parts," the set operations of "union" and "intersection" have very different properties than those of the familiar arithmetic operations of addition and multiplication. If children think of addition as joining, notice that joining the previously described set of 5 poker chips with another set of 2 poker chips, 1 of which is red will produce a set in which 3 of the 7 chips are red.

The procedure for adding fractions is based on their nature as magnitude numbers, those that arise in measurement contexts. Fractions to be added must refer to the *same* subdivision of the underlying unit because we can only add the same *kinds* of things. This is the reason we have to express the fractions in terms of a common denominator, in spite of the complicated and inconvenient nature of the process. Because of the temptation to add the numerators and add the denominators, it would be better not to introduce the set model until after children have had considerable experience in addition and subtraction of fractions that originate in measurement contexts.

Algebraic Fractions

When so many school children seem to have no understanding of meaning for numerical fractions, as documented by the Siegler and Lortie-Forgues article cited earlier in this chapter, it is hardly surprising that such students find algebraic fractions even more troublesome. It is once again the focus on counting and lack of attention to the "continuous" aspect of measurement settings that make it hard for children to develop useful intuitions of fractions.

There are also language issues. Recalling the many different meanings for the word "term" and the use of letters to represent either variables or constants shown in chapter 1, we can see that early work in algebra must fill in the gaps created for students who have simply learned arithmetic as a set of "how to do it" procedures. Algebra requires the recognition of generalizations based on meaningful connections and structures, and many children who are competent with procedures have not been prepared to make the transition to the abstractions needed in order to make sense of algebra.

The fraction bar and the slash (/)

One issue in the context of fractions that are expressed in terms of symbols as "placeholders" for numbers emerged after the invention of typewriters, when people found it convenient to use a "slash" in place of a fraction bar in order to fit the fraction on a single line of typescript. However, it is important to understand that the fraction bar also indicates a grouping, and we cannot simply replace $\frac{a+2b}{2}$ by $a+2b/2$, since the notation using the slash means that only the 2b is to be divided by 2, whereas the fraction bar form means that it is the sum of a and $2b$ that must be divided by 2. The price of fitting the fraction on a single line is the need to insert parentheses to indicate the grouping that was part of the fraction bar notation: *(a+2b)/2.*

Chapter 3
The Dangers of Oversimplification

Albert Einstein:
"Everything should be as simple as possible, but no simpler."

Geometric terminology in the primary grades

Language, as used in geometry, has always been a troubling issue. Consider Euclid's definition of a *point*, the fundamental entity of point-set geometry: "A point is that which hath no part."

The problem is that this definition only tells us that a point has no *size*, but it fails to tell us what it *is*: a location. When young children have to deal with points in geometry, what they see are marks that do have size. However, the confusion increases when geometric examples presented to young children oversimplify and distort the actual meanings of the language they are supposedly being taught.

For example, one goal is to teach meanings for the words "circle," "square," "triangle," and "rectangle." Figure 3.1 is typical of what appears in the teaching materials for the early grades: the only triangles shown are equilateral, and the only rectangles pictured are like classically proportioned "golden rectangles."

(Figure 3.1)

It is important to show young children a variety of shapes, so they can see that while all circles have the same shape and can differ only in size (and the same is true for squares), triangles and rectangles come in many shapes as well as many sizes. Furthermore, a square is a special rectangle, a rectangle with all sides equal in length. It is not necessary to mislead – and thereby confuse – young learners by avoiding these realities. This kind of misdirection is also seen in higher grades when the parallelogram is introduced without calling attention to the fact that a rectangle is a special parallelogram, just as a square is a special rectangle. There seems to be a belief that young children are not capable of understanding inclusive terminology when it involves geometry, although I have yet to meet a kindergarten child who does not understand that cats and dogs are animals.

It is also worth noting that in the 1990s, the University of Chicago School Mathematics Project published English translations of Russian school mathematics textbooks, as well as books explaining the importance of geometry in the early school curriculum. Volume seven of Soviet Studies in Mathematics Education, *Geometry in Grades 1-4*, shows how children can acquire important understandings from the very beginning of geometry exposure. By building shapes out of sticks and modeling clay, students can see, for example, that a pair of short sticks of matching length and a pair of longer sticks of matching length can be joined to form a rectangle or a parallelogram or a kite. It is also easier for children with this kind of experience to understand that a parallelogram with a pair of opposite angles that are acute, if constructed with those sticks, will have the same perimeter but NOT the same area as the rectangle made with those identical sticks. Figure 3.2 shows a rectangle, a parallelogram and a kite, all constructed with the kind of sticks described in the previous sentence.

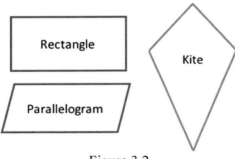

Figure 3.2

This kind of exploration provides invaluable preparation for the eventual mastery of all the formulae for perimeter, area, and volume students must eventually learn. Instead of mindlessly memorizing the area formulas for rectangles and parallelograms (A = l x w and A = b x h), students who understand that a rectangle is actually a parallelogram with right angles can see that the two formulas represent a difference of focus, but carry the same information. Notice that if we recognize that the rectangle shown in Figure 3.2 is also a parallelogram, the base of this parallelogram is what was described as length for a rectangle, while what was called the height of the parallelogram was considered the width of the rectangle. My middle school students found it very interesting to construct a rectangle with flexible corner connections and "squash" it into a parallelogram while considering what was happening to the area enclosed by the figure.

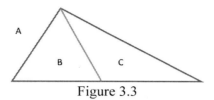

Figure 3.3

Another important reason to provide early, physical experiences in geometry is also shown in the Russian textbooks, where children are shown pictures such as the one in Figure 3.3 and guided with questions such as:

- How many triangles can you find in this diagram?
- If A is the area of the undivided triangle, and the two inner triangles have areas B and C, do you see that A = B + C?

In spite of the apparent belief that the children will learn the true meanings of geometric relationships and terminology when they are older and "more ready," school curricula provide little guidance to correct the misunderstandings created by the oversimplifications introduced in kindergarten and the early grades, and many adults do not seem to understand that a square is also a rectangle and a parallelogram.

Another advantage of the Russian curriculum shown in the University of Chicago publications is that it prepares students to grasp the idea of using symbols to express relationships that can be seen as qualitative as well as quantitative and helps them to see algebra as a language with which to describe such relationships. That curriculum was successfully implemented (on a small scale) by Jean Schmittau about 30 years ago in upstate New York. The interested reader will find the reference in the list at the end of this volume.

In contrast, when the approach to algebra is focused on finding values for unknown quantities, it is easy to lose sight of the need to establish and express the connections that exist among the various parts of what is being examined. If it's true that "a picture is worth a thousand words," it is also worth showing students the geometric aspects of algebraic formulas such as the square of a binomial, $(a + b)^2 = a^2 + 2ab + b^2$, and the Pythagorean Theorem (Figures 3.4 and 3.5). Perhaps fewer students would find algebra so difficult if they could see these "algebra formulas" as statements about geometric area relationships.

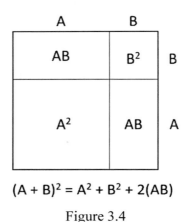

$$(A + B)^2 = A^2 + B^2 + 2(AB)$$

Figure 3.4

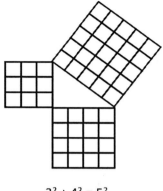

$$3^2 + 4^2 = 5^2$$

Figure 3.5

The operations of arithmetic

It comes as a surprise to many adults that addition does not necessarily require joining, subtraction does not have to involve taking anything away, and multiplication need not have anything to do with repeated addition. Unfortunately, these are often the only characterizations presented for those arithmetic operations, at least in the early grades. One reason so many children have trouble solving "story problems" is that many of the "stories" don't fit the only meaning the children have been given for the operations of arithmetic.

Consider the following scenarios:

- Sam is 3 years older than his sister Sophie. If Sophie is 5 years old, how old is Sam?

- I want to buy a toy that costs $18, but I only have $12. How much more money do I need?

It is vitally important to help young children understand that the operations of arithmetic have many different interpretations, and it is a disservice to students to oversimplify addition and subtraction by only presenting them, respectively, as joining and "taking away," since there are many other possible situations that require those operations. We create serious difficulties for students if the only meaning we offer for addition is joining and for subtraction is taking away.

Children are often taught to use "keywords" to solve story problems in a counterproductive attempt to make such problems "easier." The idea behind this strategy is that instead of trying to understand the situation that is presented, the child only needs to look for "keywords" and no thinking is required. We need to recognize the serious harm that is done when children are led to believe that thinking is not important when doing mathematics and that all they need to know is "how to do it."

Focusing on "keywords" also misleads the child into believing that a "keyword" always implies the same action. For example, believing that "more" implies addition can produce many wrong answers – notice that in the second scenario above, where the word "more" appears, subtraction is needed to answer the question asked.

We need to provide a broader view to enable young students to recognize that there are many different kinds of questions whose answers are found by adding or subtracting. One significant set of situations that gets little, if any, attention in the early grades is comparison. This is rather surprising, since young children are very aware of life situations in which one child might have more of something desirable than another. In fact, comparison is just as evident and easy for children to understand as joining or taking away.

The situation becomes even worse for the operations of multiplication and division. Elementary school mathematics textbooks routinely introduce multiplication as meaning repeated addition, and no other interpretation is offered. Of course, this leaves the learner unable to make sense of computations such as ½ x ¾ multiplication by zero, or multiplication of two negative numbers, like (-2) x (-6). Notice that "repeated addition" does not apply to the scenario below.

- Jim found ¾ of a pizza in the refrigerator, and he ate ½ of what he found. What part of a whole pizza did Jim eat?

One reason for our apparent inability to offer other meanings for multiplication in the primary grades has come from our failure to make use of the numerical aspects of geometric relationships. It is important to recall that, as noted in Chapter 1, recognition of the existence of "incommensurable" lengths in a simple isosceles right-angled triangle led the early Greek mathematicians to distinguish between "multitude" numbers and "magnitude" numbers. The early Euclidean geometers developed an extensive theory of proportionality in which multiplication and division are used to compare geometric entities such as length and area. While young children do not have the skills and understanding needed for deep work with proportionality, early qualitative geometry experiences can help them understand multiplication as having meanings other than repeated addition.

For example, well before the introduction of any formula, such as that for the area of a rectangle as length x width, children should have enough hands-on experience to understand that the factors, length and width, are one-dimensional, while the product area, is two-dimensional. Recall the discussion in Chapter 2 about the need to acknowledge that most of the numbers that appear in formulas are "denominate numbers," whose values depend as much on the unit as the number.

Furthermore, the factors and the product are *fundamentally different kinds of geometric objects*, and are measured with different kinds of units. We need to give enough attention to the differences between units such as meters and square meters to help children understand that the product of two *measured* numbers has a unit that is *not* the same as *either* of the factors.

While it is indeed possible to visualize the area of a square or a rectangle whose sides appear to have whole-number lengths as covered by unit squares, to conform to a repeated addition model, this is very contrived. An *idealized* square may have a whole-number side length, but the side length of an actual geometric square is a magnitude rather than a whole number, and "repeated addition" is not adequate to explain why the area of a parallelogram may be found by multiplying the length of the base by the height.

There are many other situations involving multiplication that have nothing to do with repeated addition. For example, we frequently make multiplicative comparisons such as "twice as many" and "one-third as much as…"; students encounter change of scale with maps in social studies as well as stretching or shrinking: "A strip of elastic sewn into the waistband of a skirt is pulled to twice its original length when the skirt is worn. If the skirt fits a 30-inch waist, what was the original length of the elastic?" Eventually students will deal with the use of combinations such as "If Peter has 5 shirts and 3 pairs of pants, how many different ways could he be dressed?"

Once integers (signed numbers) appear in the curriculum, the idea that multiplication is nothing but repeated addition becomes useless, and the novice who is trying to make sense of mathematics is left with little recourse other than imitation and memorization in order to survive. This makes it even more important that we help children achieve a deeper understanding of the variety of interpretations for the operations of arithmetic.

As an aside note, many students do not seem to recognize that the word "of" in some of the story problems can imply multiplication. Perhaps it is because this little preposition is not usually seen in whole-number contexts. We might say we have "6 fours" or "6 groups of four" and everyone seems to know that this means that there are 6 x 4 or 24 objects. However, seeing "⅔ of ⅜" as ⅔ x ⅜ seems to be less natural. It's important to help students understand the variety of geometric and arithmetical situations that cannot be seen in terms of repeated addition but do imply multiplication.

Chapter 4
The Importance of Context

Alfred Marshall:
> "In common use almost every word has many shades of meaning, and therefore needs to be interpreted by the context."

The power of mathematics is often due to its ability to transcend context, but in order to interpret a mathematical result we have to return to the context of the original question or problem. If we believe, or teach, that "there is only one correct answer" we ignore context, often inappropriately.

For example, the question, "How many tens are there in 634?" is ambiguous. The answer could be "3" or "63." It depends on whether the context requires the answer to state how many hundreds, tens, and units are given by the numeral 634 or to tell how many sets of ten items can be formed if we have 634 items.

The number line

The number line is the basis of many vitally important mathematical concepts. It is invaluable in establishing an understanding of negative numbers in terms of reflecting the number line over the origin, and it is the basis of graphing and analytical geometry. Our North American curricula usually introduce the number line in the primary grades, where it is used to illustrate stories about frogs or bunnies hopping along the number line in steps with a specified whole-number length, and the whole numbers are identified with marked points as shown.

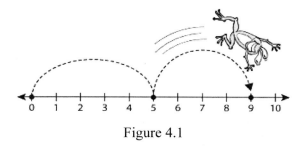

Figure 4.1

This example is meant to help children understand why $5 + 4 = 9$. However, if the only context children have is whole numbers, the number line can be very confusing. One serious issue is that in order to show an interval of a given length, say three units, it takes an extra point, one more than the length of the unit. For example, using only whole numbers, we can show many intervals three units long: one from 0 to 3 that shows 0, 1, 2, and 3; another from 1 to 4 that shows 1, 2, 3, and 4; another from 2 to 5 that shows 2, 3, 4, and 5; and so on. But it seems more natural for many young children to count *points* on the number line instead of *intervals* – since they only have information about whole numbers in terms of counting, this is not surprising. The fact that counting the demarcation points rather than intervals is a natural human tendency also appears in the conventions used for intervals in music. A musical interval that spans C-D-E (or do-re-mi) is called a "third" in music, even though it only covers two tones, because it takes three *notes* (or points on the scale) to define the *interval*.

It is not uncommon to see incorrect answers in textbooks for problems that fail to take this issue into account. Here is such an example: "The highway department of your county wants to place markers at quarter-mile intervals along two miles of a highway to make it possible for motorists to verify the accuracy of the odometer of their cars. How many markers do they have to order?" The answer provided was 8. Of course, there are 8 quarter-mile segments in the stretch of highway, but 9 markers are required since unless there is a marker placed at the start of the marked section (the zero point) the driver will not know when the car enters the marked section of the highway.

We may create a serious problem for children by giving them their first introduction to the number line in the context of whole numbers. Unless they have had enough experience with measurement to understand the number line as a generalization of the ruler, it is all too easy to form a mindset that places the focus on the discrete points identified by the whole numbers. Ultimately, students need to be able to recognize that the number line is a continuous entity rather than separated points. Every high school teacher I know has had to work hard to help students "unlearn" the notion that there is nothing of value on the number line between the whole-number points. Curriculum designers need to consider the disadvantages of premature use of the number line for whole-number addition and subtraction.

Since the number line is continuous, there are infinitely many numbers between the whole-number markings. In fact, it is the intervals (i.e., copies of the unit) rather than points that are being counted. To put it another way, the number line is an entity that belongs in the world of "magnitudes." While we can also make use of it in the world of "multitudes," we do this by ignoring the underlying fundamental properties for the sake of convenience. However, I would argue that if the goal is to teach addition and subtraction of whole numbers, it may be counterproductive to use a continuous model when discrete models are available.

The mathematics education community has actually been offered a very effective way to overcome the problems discussed in the previous paragraphs. Richard R. Skemp[1] has developed activities for children in which he used what he termed the "number track" with young children before asking them to use the number line. The "number track" places the focus on counting intervals rather than points on a number line, by placing the whole numbers 1, 2, 3… within the interval rather than at the point where intervals begin or end, thereby avoiding the kind of cognitive dissonance discussed above.

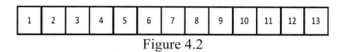

Figure 4.2

If we were to provide for students to have adequate experience with the use of rulers for measuring, they would be able to recognize the distinction between the intervals and the points that indicate how many intervals occupy the space that begins at 0. It is vitally important that the number line be seen as something that displays real numbers, and the rational numbers be seen as a subset of the real numbers, if the number line is to be helpful rather than simply a mysterious mathematical artifact. As discussed in the first two chapters, this requires a direct approach to the distinction between the kinds of numbers that describe discrete and continuous aspects of nature.

Eventually the number line will be extended to the left to show the negative numbers, as shown in Figure 4.3, and students will have to learn to do arithmetic with the integers shown in Figure 4.3, as well as with the rational and real numbers that lie between the marked integer points. It is important to keep in mind that the early curriculum has most likely failed to provide rich enough interpretations for the

---

[1] Skemp, Richard. The Reflective Educator.
https://davidwees.com/content/difference-between-instrumental-and-relational-understanding/
See also Skemp, Richard. http://www.skemp.org.uk/

operations of arithmetic, as discussed in the previous chapter. Students need to learn about the variety of real-world contexts that give rise to such numbers and they must also be aware of many more meanings for the operations of arithmetic than those traditionally seen when they were only doing whole-number arithmetic.

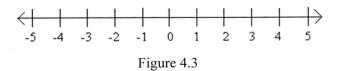

Figure 4.3

We don't always say what we mean

Other language issues arise because of discrepancies between the commonly accepted meaning of a word and the formal definitions made in mathematics. Here are some examples:

- Spoken language, what we say orally, can fail to satisfy the meaning stated by the actual definition of a symbol used for the intended concept. For example, "the square root of 9" is defined as any number that produces 9 when it is multiplied by itself. This means that the square root of 9 can be either +3 or -3, usually written as ±3. However, the symbol "√9" is actually defined formally as the *principal* (i.e., positive) square root of 9, namely 3. However, what is usually *said* when the symbol "√9" is seen is "the square root of 9," not "the principal square root of 9."

- Teachers often use a sheet of paper to illustrate a rectangle. What is not usually mentioned is that it is the *boundary* of the paper that is the "rectangle," while the sheet of paper itself is a model of a rectangular region. While this may not be a serious issue for young children, there are times when it is important to distinguish between a polygon and a polygonal region. An empty picture frame might serve as a better example of what the definition of a rectangle actually means.

- The geometric solids (e.g. cube, sphere, cone, polyhedron…) are actually hollow, according to their definitions. For example, a sphere is defined as the set of points in space at a given distance from a fixed point (the center). A sphere together with the points in its interior is called a "spherical region." In general, any geometric "solid" is defined as the set of points that form the *boundary* of the figure, which means that it is actually hollow rather than "solid."

- In mathematics, the definition of a *curve* is "the path traced out by a moving point." Note that this means that a curve may in fact be straight, which may not accord with our everyday usage of this word. In fact, without additional context, it is not clear whether or not the word "line" implies "straightness."

Chapter 5
Psychological Impact of Language and Notation

Karl Friedrich Gauss (about imaginary numbers):

> "That this subject has hitherto been surrounded by mysterious obscurity is to be attributed largely to an ill adapted notation. If, for example, +1, -1, and the square root of -1 had been called direct, inverse, and lateral units, instead of positive, negative, and imaginary (or even impossible), such an obscurity would have been out of the question.

Gauss lived from 1777 to 1855, but we can see that he foresaw that the language "imaginary number" would promote the idea that they are not useful for physical or "real-world" phenomena.

As we have noted earlier, every number is an abstraction, an idea, rather than something concrete, which means that any number can be considered to be "imaginary." When negative numbers were first introduced, they were also considered to be useless. It was the banking industry that helped people understand that in fact there is a "real" and important meaning for negative numbers, in terms of describing a debt. For number lines, the concepts of positive and negative numbers are used to designate a direction from what is often an arbitrary choice of a center, or "zero" location. In measuring temperature, there are different locations for zero in the Fahrenheit and Celsius scales. In geography, positions above or below sea level are expressed in terms of positive and negative numbers.

As mathematics, physics, and technology advanced, people eventually began to understand that there are valid real-world meanings for what were, at first, called "imaginary numbers." The mathematics used in understanding the phenomena of electricity and magnetism depends heavily on the use of "complex" numbers, having the form a + bi, the sum of a "real" part and an "imaginary" part. Unfortunately, the "imaginary" terminology is now entrenched, although we all know that electricity and magnetism are very "real" phenomena. This requires mathematics educators to make sure that their students are aware of the anachronisms represented by such language.

Psychological issues may be implicated in the problem many students seem to have regarding the terms Greatest Common Factor (GCF) and Least Common Multiple (LCM). Both terms appear in the context of fraction arithmetic and many students seem to have trouble connecting the appropriate term to the concept to which it applies. For any given number, a "factor" is a divisor, and hence must be smaller, or at most, equal to that number. For two or more numbers, the GCF is the *largest* number that divides evenly into all of them. Notice, however, that the GCF cannot be larger than the smallest of the numbers in the set. On the other hand, a "multiple" of any number is the result of multiplying that number by a whole number, and a "common" multiple of a set of numbers is a number that can be found by multiplying each number in the set by some whole number. The LCM is the *smallest* number which is a multiple of each number in the set, and so it can never be smaller than the largest of those numbers. It seems that the psychological issue comes from triggering on the first word in each phrase – the "G" of GCF seems to trigger a sense that we need a large number, and overcomes the more important fact that this number is a *factor* and so cannot be larger than any member of the set.

Consider the following counterproductive (and counterintuitive in today's world) language:

- Real numbers: as previously discussed, every number is an abstraction and therefore not "real." This is simply language left over from an age where we did not yet understand mathematics as anything more than a tool for dealing with the physical world and were also unaware that many real-world phenomena are most accurately and usefully described using numbers that are not included in the set of "real" numbers.

- "Improper" fractions: this anachronistic terminology comes from an era where commerce was the most important context for computation and algebra was in its infancy. A fraction such as $\frac{7}{3}$ was designated as "improper" because for commerce we want to see the value as a "mixed number," namely 2⅓, where the whole number part is explicitly shown. However, whenever we need to multiply or divide with this value, the "improper" form is the one that is most useful since carrying out multiplication using the mixed number form is cumbersome and slow.

- "Reducing" a fraction does not result in a smaller value for the fraction. While the numbers in the numerator and denominator may be "reduced," the value of the number represented by the fraction is unchanged.

- The "imaginary" unit is $i = \sqrt{-1}$ and, as Gauss observed, we have given the concept of an "imaginary number" a mysterious obscurity, simply by using the word "imaginary" in the way it is discussed.

Chapter 6
When We Let Convenience Overrule Fundamental Issues

Proverb:
"Every convenience brings its own inconveniences along with it."

Arbitrary conventions in the context of numbers

What follows are some illustrations to show that the verbal and symbolic language in mathematics has many aspects that are neither logical nor consistent. While it is undoubtedly true that every language has such problems, in mathematics it is repeatedly claimed that everything *is* logical and consistent. Math educators must recognize that such claims cannot be justified and instead we should help students recognize and deal with the reality of the many arbitrary and inconsistent conventions actually used.

Here are some examples:

Sequential constructions

- In our base-ten numbers system, digits written in sequence arise from a kind of shorthand involving both multiplication and addition. For example, 723 means $7 \cdot 100 + 2 \cdot 10 + 3$.

- When numbers and letters, or just letters are written sequentially (for example, $5x$ or xy), they are to be multiplied.

- A "mixed number," which is a sequence of a whole number and a fraction, is a shorthand for adding a fraction to a whole number: $5\frac{1}{3} = 5 + \frac{1}{3}$

The "order of operations" conventions

In view of the reputation of mathematics as the bastion of logical reasoning, it is actually very sobering to recognize how often we ignore the logical requirements and create much confusion for the learner. Here are some examples of expressions for which pure logic produces more than one possible correct evaluation. In each case, how can the learner know which result is "correct"?

- $12 - 5 - 3$ (Is the correct value 10 or 4?)

- $16 \div 4 \div 2$ (Is the correct value 8 or 2?)

- -4^2 (Is the correct answer 16 or -16?)

- $36 + 9 \div 3 \times 5$ (Is the correct answer 75 or 51 or 3?)

The fact is that in the absence of grouping symbols, there is no logical way to determine the correct value in these examples. For the first two expressions, involving sequential subtractions or divisions, the issue arises because the operations of arithmetic are *binary* (only two numbers can be combined at a time), and subtraction and division both lack the associative property. When more than two numbers have to be combined using subtraction or division, the order in which the first two numbers are combined makes a difference. By contrast, the associative property holds for addition and multiplication, so it is not necessary to indicate the order in which first two numbers are chosen.

For the third, example, the issue is about whether the exponent is to be applied to 4 or -4.

For the last, there are three operations, each of which is binary, and the order in which any two adjacent numbers are combined using the indicated operation does make a difference.

Logically, unless grouping symbols are provided, all the expressions shown fail to have a well-defined value. Since people are apparently unwilling to go to the extra trouble of providing the symbols that would remove the ambiguities, we have adopted a set of "order of operations conventions," usually abbreviated as PEMDAS and presented to students with the mnemonic "Please Excuse My Dear Aunt Sally," which instructs us to proceed, working from left to right, to first perform any operations in Parentheses, then apply any Exponent to the number immediately preceding it, then do all Multiplications or Divisions, from left to right, and then all Additions and Subtractions, from left to right.

Unfortunately, these conventions, usually presented as "rules," never receive enough attention, and the instructional materials fail to mention that they are not based on logic, but have been adopted in order to not have to do the extra work required to actually provide the intended groupings. Notice also that when children are taught the usual algorithms for addition and subtraction, it is constantly stressed that they must work in the opposite direction, from right to left, in order to "more efficiently" handle the "carrying" and "borrowing" procedures. If we want to continue to value expediency over clarity, let us at least be honest about it, and ensure that students have enough experience to master the rules in a non-punitive way.

Order of operations for calculators

In view of the now ubiquitous use of calculators for most routine computation, it's also important for people to keep their wits about them while using these devices to handle the time-consuming details. Most people would be surprised to learn how often entry errors and lack of awareness of the appropriate order of key strokes can produce wrong answers, even when the user knows what he or she is doing. Banks generally require the use of machines that will print out a tape so that errors can be found – as mentioned in Chapter 2, one surprising result noted on such tapes is that we often reverse digits when entering multi-digit numbers, so that an entry that should have been 85 might be entered as 58. Another frequent source of error can come from lack of awareness of a calculator's built-in "order of operations." In one college pre-calculus class I taught I noticed that almost half the students had the same incorrect answer for one of the assigned problems, whose solution involved a fraction like this: $\frac{124+44}{2}$. The correct result is 84, but about half the students gave the same wrong answer: 146. This was because when keying the computation into the calculator, the students with the wrong answer had not pressed the "=" key before pressing the "÷" key and the calculator had only divided 44 by 2 and then added that result to 124 to get 146. We had a fruitful discussion about the need to be sufficiently attentive to recognize that the result of such a computation has to be less than 100, and to recognize that the 146 that appeared on the calculator must therefore be wrong.

Cancellation

The literal meaning of the word "cancel" involves making something disappear. It seems that many children come to believe that one of the "rules" they have been taught in the context of fractions is that if a number or symbol appears in both the numerator and denominator, they can "cancel" by simply crossing it out. What seems not to have been understood is that this kind of "simplification" is only valid – that is, it doesn't change the <u>value</u> of the fraction – when it is the result of <u>dividing</u> the numerator and denominator by the same number. For example, while $\frac{2a}{2b} = \frac{a}{b}$, $\frac{2+a}{2+b} \neq \frac{a}{b}$. It can be useful if the teacher simply stops using the word "cancel" in this context and instead uses language that emphasizes the process of dividing the numerator and denominator by the same number to simplify the fraction. In the previous chapter, it was mentioned that this is sometimes described as reducing the fraction to lowest terms, and that use of the word "reduce" can also have a counterproductive effect.

The term "cancel" is also used in the context of algebraic equations, where we have two cancellation laws, one for addition and one for multiplication:

If x + a = y + a, then x = y
If ax = ay, then x = y

Again, in the first case the same number is being subtracted from both sides of the equation while in the second, both sides of the equation are being divided by the same number. It does not seem to be helpful to use the word "cancel" at all.

Chapter 7
The Joy of Math

The most important reason to help students master the language aspects of mathematics is that "speaking the language" is key to understanding, and mathematical empowerment can provide many opportunities to experience what I call the "AHA!" moment. The need to understand the world in which we live seems to be part of our evolutionary heritage, undoubtedly a vital survival skill, and it has certainly been my own experience that each new deep understanding about the world comes with the feeling of transcendence.

It seems to have been Galileo who first articulated the idea that the story of the universe is written in the language of mathematics, and as time goes on, there has been more and more agreement with this point of view. In 1960, the Physicist Eugene Wigner published an article with the title *The Unreasonable Effectiveness of Mathematics in the Natural Sciences* that made a big impact and is frequently quoted.

I was lucky to have had an "AHA!" moment early in my schooling that made me aware of the ability of arithmetic to produce that kind of excitement. It actually happened in connection with a story we were reading, probably in grade 2 or 3. The story was about a boy (I'll call him Bill, I have no recollection of his name) who didn't have much athletic ability and was often sad because he would always be one of the last chosen when teams were being formed for sports activities.

However, the teacher in this story held "math bees" from time to time, where two teams were formed and lined up on opposite sides of the room, and each of the children took turns asking a question to be answered by a member of the opposing team. In the story, Bill was always the first to be chosen as a team member for the math bees; his team always won because Bill knew the "secret of the nines." All our school notebooks in those days had arithmetic facts on the back cover, including the addition and multiplication tables, and tables of weights and measures. I wondered what could possibly be meant by "the secret of the nines" and looked at the back of my notebook, and found the column under "9" in the multiplication table:

x	1	2	3	4	5	6	7	8	9
1	1	2	3	4	5	6	7	8	9
2	2	4	6	8	10	12	14	16	18
3	3	6	9	12	15	18	21	24	27
4	4	8	12	16	20	24	28	32	36
5	5	10	15	20	25	30	35	40	45
6	6	12	18	24	30	36	42	48	54
7	7	14	21	28	35	42	49	56	63
8	8	16	24	32	40	48	56	64	72
9	9	18	27	36	45	54	63	72	81

It didn't take long for the pattern to jump out – the first digit is one less than the multiplier and two digits always add up to 9. AHA! I had found "the secret of the nines."

Of course, there are also opportunities for "AHA!" experiences in other settings. I once took a short set of art classes, and when the lesson involved drawing trees with foliage, the instructor suggested that instead of looking at the lines, we should try to look at the spaces. I felt as though I was seeing the world quite differently after that lesson, and another important realization soon evolved: I could no longer remember how I had seen the world before this experience. This was a very useful experience for a mathematics educator about how easy it is to forget what was originally found hard to understand about something, once it is seen from a different perspective.

If humans are in fact deeply motivated to understand how and why things happen and if Galileo was correct, then it would seem that mathematics can provide experiences rich in awe and wonder. I have certainly found this to be a source of inspiration myself, and I have also seen many of my students enjoy those moments of discovery. For example, when I taught mathematics in middle school, many students experienced the "AHA!" when they grasped the idea that between ANY two fractions, no matter how close they are on the number line, you can insert as many more fractions as you like – an experience about "infinitely many" numbers in a very small space. But such experiences can only happen if we move beyond the outmoded idea that learning mathematics is simply a matter of knowing "how to do it" and help our students see meaning in what is being learned.

Anyone who really wants to understand how the world works will find it easier if they know mathematics. The ancient "riddles" of the Zeno Paradoxes as well as some classical philosophical questions such as "If a tree falls in the forest and no one is around, does it make a sound?" can all be answered using mathematics and the math-dependent sciences. Phenomena such as how rainbows happen, or why heavy airplanes can fly, or why we see lightning before we hear the thunder in a thunderstorm all use mathematics to answer the "how" or the "why." It's also fascinating to learn that once a new aspect of mathematics is developed to try to solve a specific kind of problem, it is eventually found to be useful in a different setting.

We need to empower children with mathematical understanding for many reasons. Some of these involve helping them to become successful in fields depending on expertise in what are referred to as STEM (Science, Technology, Engineering, Mathematics), where there seems to be such a shortage of qualified Americans that we have to import people educated in other countries. But it is equally important to help our young people experience the satisfaction that comes from understanding the nature of our world.

Notes and References

Butterworth, Brian. *The Mathematical Brain.*
http://www.mathematicalbrain.com/

Carey, S. (1998). *Knowledge of number: its Evolution and Ontogeny.* Science, 282 (5389), 641–642.

Dehaene, S. (2011). *The Number Sense: How the Mind Creates Mathematics* (Rev. and updated ed.). New York, NY, US: Oxford University Press.

Devlin, Keith (2008) *It Ain't No Repeated Addition.* Devlin's Angle, Mathematical Association of America, June 2008.

Siegler and Lortie-Forgues. Hard Lessons: Why Rational Number Arithmetic is So Difficult for So Many People. *Sage Journals.* http://journals.sagepub.com/doi/abs/10.1177/096372141770 0129